EXPLORE

ELECTRICITY!

Carmella Van Vleet

Illustrated by Bryan Stone

More science titles in the **Explore Your World!** Series

Check out more titles at www.nomadpress.net

Nomad Press
A division of Nomad Communications
10 9 8 7 6 5 4 3

ISBN: 978-1-61930-180-1

Educational Consultant, Marla Conn

Questions regarding the ordering of this book should be addressed to
Nomad Press
2456 Christian St.
White River Junction, VT 05001
www.nomadpress.net

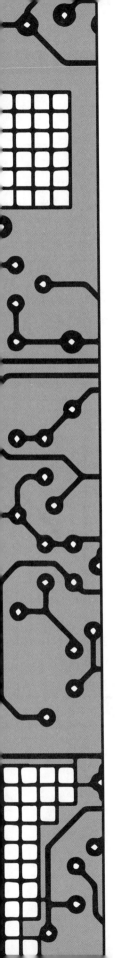

CONTENTS

TIMELINE

600s BCE: Thales of Miletus recognizes that rubbing wool or fur on amber causes static electricity.

1600s: William Gilbert invents the versorium, an instrument that can detect electrical charges.

1837: The first electric motors are built.

1830: Hans Christian Oersted and Michael Faraday discover the principles of electromagnetism. James Maxwell later combines these principles into a single theory.

1879: Thomas Edison invents a filament that makes light bulbs an option for households.

1880: Edison Electric Light Company is founded.

1883: James Wimshurst invents a machine that builds up an electric charge.

1940s: Electronic computers are invented and the first televisions go on sale.

1895: Nikola Tesla invents a system that alternates electrical current.

1895: Niagra Falls becomes the first large-scale hydro-powered electric plant.

1900–1940: Electric motors are used in appliances like vacuum cleaners, washing machines, televisions, electric freezers, and air conditioners.

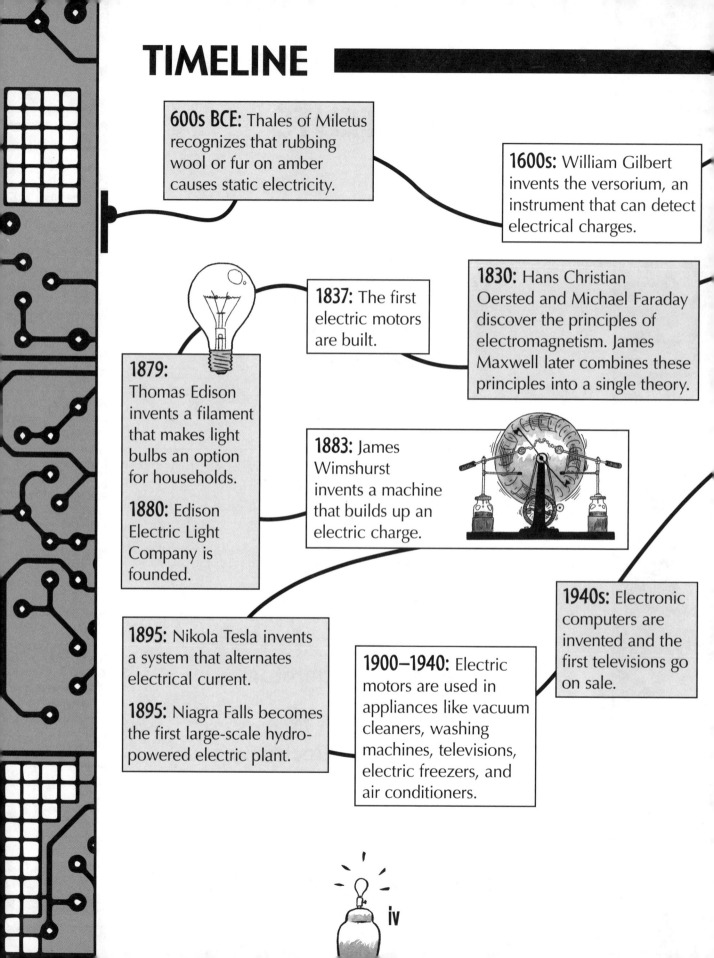

TIMELINE

1745: German inventor Ewald von Kleist and Pieter van Musschenbroek of Holland separately discover a device that can store an electrical charge. This becomes known as the Leyden jar.

1750: Benjamin Franklin begins experimenting with electricity. He later flies a kite in a storm to prove that lightning is an electrical charge.

1800: Alessandro Volta invents the first chemical battery.

1780: Luigi Galvani demonstrates that an animal's nerves have an electrical basis.

1950s: Grace Murray Hopper is instrumental in the development of COBOL, one of the first computer languages. She had earlier coined the terms *computer bug* and *debugging* to describe fixing a computer problem.

1990s: Compact fluorescent bulbs grow in popularity, as does wind, solar, hydro and nuclear power.

2000s: Laptop computers, cell phones, and tablets are all common household items. Smaller batteries that deliver more energy make this technology possible.

1951: The first nuclear reactor is built and used to generate energy.

1960s: Transistors make portable radios possible.

FUTURE: Super tiny robots called nanobots may be used in science and medicine.

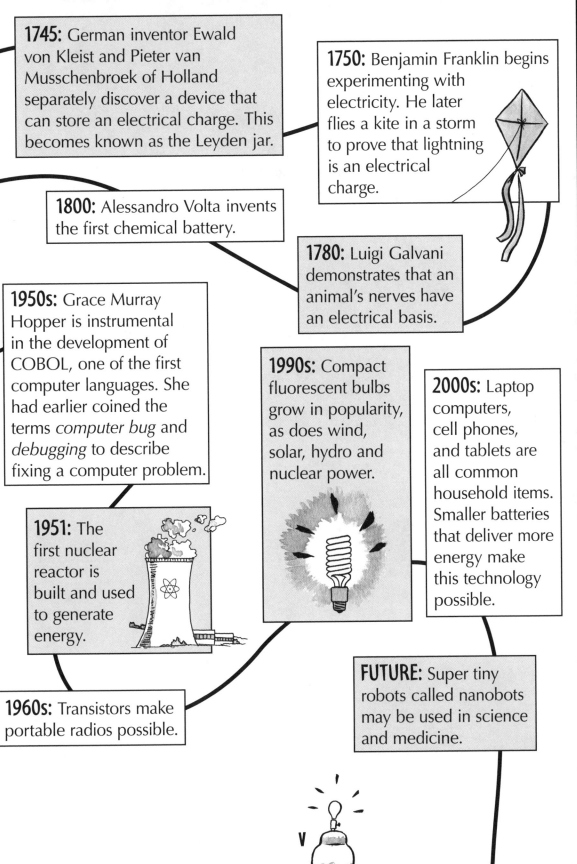

For my nieces and nephews and my little buddy
Sebastian—who light up the world.

Let's Explore Electricity

What is the first thing you did when you woke up this morning? You probably turned on a light or went to the kitchen for breakfast. Maybe someone made you pancakes on the stove or toast in the toaster. Did you watch television or listen to music or use a computer? All of these things required **electricity**.

- - - - - - - - - - - - - - - - - -

Electricity is a kind of natural **energy**. Some people think Thomas Edison or Benjamin Franklin invented it. But nobody really invented electricity. It's been around since the earth was formed.

WORDS to KNOW

electricity: a form of energy caused by the movement of tiny particles. It provides power for lights, appliances, video games, and many other electric devices.

energy: the ability to do things, to work.

WORDS to KNOW

BCE: put after a date, BCE stands for Before the Common Era and counts down to zero. BCE is a non-religious term that means the same thing as BC.

amber: a piece of fossilized tree sap or resin.

static electricity: the buildup of an electric charge on the surface of an object.

CE: put after a date, CE stands for Common Era and counts up from zero. CE is a non-religious term that means the same thing as AD.

Thousands of years ago people knew about electricity because they could see it in action. But they didn't understand it.

For example, the ancient Greek scientist Thales of Miletus lived from 625 to 547 **BCE**. He knew that if you rub a piece of **amber** with wool or fur it attracts lightweight objects like feathers and dust.

Maybe you have seen something similar happen when you rub a balloon on your head. The balloon will stick on the wall without falling. Today we call this **static electricity**. The ancient Greeks had no name for it.

Pliny the Elder (23–79 **CE**), an ancient Greek scientist, knew that being shocked by an electric catfish could help numb a person's pain. Later on, many scientists around the world studied electricity and how it works. But it's only been in the last few hundred years that we've learned how to make the power of electricity useful to us.

DID YOU KNOW?

The word *electricity* comes from the ancient Greek word *elektron*. This was the Greek word for amber.

WORDS to KNOW

charge: an amount of stored electricity.

power: electricity made available to use.

force: a push or a pull.

blackout: a loss of power.

Today our modern-day lives depend on electricity. A lot! Think about the last time you lost power at your home. It was probably hard to live without lights and the phone and the computer. Did you have to cook on a grill outside instead of on the stove or in your microwave? Maybe you used a cell phone to communicate with friends and family. But what happened when the phone lost its **charge**? No way to make a phone call. That could be very scary if you're out of power for a while and need some help.

Hey, Who Turned Out the Lights?

We can lose **power** when storms or other **forces** knock down electrical wires or equipment or when too many people are trying to use electricity at the same time. The biggest **blackout** in the world occurred on July 31, 2012, when 640 million people in India lost power. That's about 10 percent of the world's population!

WORDS to KNOW

generate: to create something.

conductor: something that electricity moves through easily, like copper wire.

insulator: a material that prevents heat, sound, or electricity from passing through it easily.

circuit: a loop that starts and finishes at the same place.

motor: a machine that turns electrical energy into motion.

generator: a device that turns motion into electricity.

resource: something that people can use.

electric current: the flow of an electrical charge through a conductor.

outlet: a device in a wall that an electric cord plugs into.

appliance: an electrical machine used in the home, such as a toaster or washing machine.

In this book, you'll explore what causes electricity and the ways it's **generated**, stored, and used. You'll learn about its power and the role it plays in our lives. You'll find out what **conductors** and **insulators** are, how **circuits** work, and the difference between a **motor** and a **generator**. You'll also explore how scientists are trying to generate Earth-friendly electricity and energy **resources**. Along the way, you'll get to do some fun projects and experiments. So get charged up and let's explore electricity!

Safety First

Electricity is a neat thing and important to our lives. But it can also be very dangerous. Coming in contact with even a small amount of electricity can burn or even kill us. This is because our muscles—including our hearts—rely on electrical signals to work. When we come in contact with a strong **electric current** outside of our bodies, it disrupts these signals. Always treat **outlets**, plugs, and electrical **appliances** with care. And remember, the activities in this book are safe as they are written. Don't be tempted to change them.

Science Journal

Thales of Miletus, the ancient Greek scientist, did simple experiments involving electricity. But we know this only because other people wrote about it. None of Thales' own books or notes survived through history. Create your own science journal to record observations and take notes. Just keep it in a safe place so your important discoveries aren't forgotten.

SUPPLIES

- brown grocery bag
- composition book
- pencil
- scissors
- newspaper
- dish or makeup sponge
- brown acrylic paint
- white glue
- duct tape (any color)
- colored markers

1 To make a fun cover for your science journal, lay the grocery bag flat on a table. Put the composition book on top of the bag and trace around it, adding about an inch around all sides (2½ centimeters).

2 Cut through both sides of the bag along the line you made. You should have two pieces of brown paper the same size.

3 Crumple up each piece of paper into a tight ball. Next, carefully unfold and smooth out the paper balls as best you can. It's okay for them still to have wrinkles.

TAP
TAP
TAP

4 Spread newspaper over your workspace. Lay the pieces of the grocery bag on the newspaper, making sure that any writing on the bags is facing down.

5 Use the sponge to dab brown paint over the paper. Try to cover the paper evenly. Let it dry.

CONTINUED ON NEXT PAGE . . .

6 Once the paper is dry, glue one piece on the front cover of the composition book. Glue the other piece on the back cover. Trim off any extra paper. If the paper is still a little too wrinkly, you can place a few heavy books on top of the journal overnight to help flatten it.

7 Cut a piece of duct tape the length of the notebook. With the notebook closed, wrap the tape down the length of the spine to create a decorative edge.

8 Have some fun decorating your science journal. First write the title across the front cover. Then think about what you want to put on the cover. You can add to the cover as you learn more about electricity in this book.

9 A scientific method worksheet is a useful tool for keeping your ideas and observations organized. The scientific method is the way scientists ask questions and then find answers. Use the inside pages to make a scientific method worksheet for each experiment.

SCIENTIFIC METHOD WORKSHEET

QUESTIONS: What is the point of this activity? What am I trying to find out? What problem am I trying to solve?

EQUIPMENT: What did I use?

METHOD: What did I do?

PREDICTIONS: What do I think will happen?

RESULTS: What actually happened? Why?

Lights Out

How much does losing power affect you? You can do this experiment during the day or wait until night if your family is willing to join in. You are allowed to use just two battery-operated devices: the clock and flashlight.

1 Begin your experiment by predicting what you will miss the most when you can't use electricity. How many things do you think you won't be able to do? Create a scientific method worksheet in your journal and write your predictions.

2 Set your alarm clock for one hour ahead. If you're doing this experiment at night, walk around your house and turn off all the lights, televisions, and computers. Turn off the heat or the air conditioner. Use the flashlight to make your way around the house safely and record your observations in your journal.

3 Next, begin your normal routine for that time of the day. Any time you discover you can't do something you'd normally do or want to do, record it in your science journal. Also note how not having electricity made your normal routines more challenging.

4 When the hour is up, notice how many times you couldn't do something because it needed electricity. Were there any surprises? Was there anything you had to do differently?

THINGS TO THINK ABOUT: Can you come up with solutions to problems caused by having no electricity? Are there other ways to cook? What's your favorite game or activity to do when the lights are out? What did other people in your family miss the most?

Switch It Up

SUPPLIES
- science journal
- pencil
- timer

This is a way to get a sense of how much you rely on electricity without even realizing it.

1 To begin, make a prediction about how many times you turn something on or off in one hour. This can mean flipping a switch, pushing a button, turning a knob, or pulling on a cord. Record your prediction in a scientific method worksheet in your journal.

2 Next, set the timer for one hour. Go about your normal routine. Each time you turn something on or off, make a mark in your journal. These marks will be your data, or scientific results.

3 When an hour is up, compare your prediction with your data. Based on your observations, how much do you rely on electricity?

4 Does your environment effect how much electricity you use? Make a prediction and try the experiment again while you're at school, a store, or the park. Test your prediction and record your data in your journal.

THINGS TO THINK ABOUT: Now that you're aware of when and why you're using electricity every day, can you find ways to cut back?

DID YOU KNOW?

Animals also carry electric charges. Some use these charges to hunt for food. The electric ray has a special muscle that acts like a battery. It sends out a shock to stun nearby creatures. And sharks have special electrical senses that help them find a tasty fish snack from miles away.

Static Electricity

Electricity is all around us. We use it every day, whether we're at home, at school, or in the car. It's hard to imagine a day without electricity. But what, exactly, is electricity? The simple answer is that electricity is a form of energy caused by the movement of tiny particles called **electrons**. But what are electrons?

Electrons are tiny particles found in **atoms**. Everything is made up of atoms. These atoms combine in different ways to make trees, computers, the air, animals, rocks—everything, including you!

WORDS to KNOW

electron: a particle in an atom that carries a negative charge. It is part of a shell moving around the center of an atom.

atom: a small particle of matter. Atoms are the extremely tiny building blocks of everything.

9

Electrons and Electricity

Some things, like gold or silver, are made of one kind of atom. But most things are made of combinations of atoms. Have you heard water called H_2O? This refers to the combination of **hydrogen** and **oxygen** atoms that make up water.

Atoms are very small bits of **matter**. They are so small we can't see them with our eyes. But everything we can touch, see, feel, smell, or taste is made of atoms. Inside an atom are even smaller particles, called **protons**, **neutrons**, and electrons. Protons and electrons carry an electric charge.

Different kinds of atoms have different numbers of these particles. Most of the time, atoms have the same number of electrons as protons. The equal amounts of negative and positive charge are in balance, or **neutral**. But sometimes, when atoms rub against each other, electrons "jump" or move from atom to atom. This jump causes a stream. And this stream is what we call electricity.

WORDS to KNOW

hydrogen: the smallest and most plentiful atom in the universe, mostly found attached to other atoms.

oxygen: a colorless gas with no smell that makes up about one-fifth of the air around us.

matter: anything that has weight and takes up space.

proton: a tiny particle inside the center of an atom that carries a positive charge.

neutron: a tiny particle inside the center of an atom that carries no charge.

neutral: not having a positive or negative charge.

Atoms are so small that about a million of them could stretch across one human hair.

If an atom has more electrons than protons it is negatively charged. That's because electrons have a negative charge and there are more of them. If an atom has fewer electrons than protons, it is positively charged. That's because protons carry a positive charge and there are more of them.

When objects have charges that are not equal, we get static electricity. This is the buildup of an electric charge on the surface of an object. The electric charge stays on the surface until it touches something with an opposite charge. Then the electricity jumps and goes back to neutral.

WORDS to KNOW

repel: to force away or apart.

A Hair-Raising Experience

Think back to a dry, cold day when you brushed your hair with a plastic brush or comb or came in from outside and pulled off a wool hat. What happened? Your hair probably stood up straight.

When you combed your hair or pulled off your hat, some electrons rubbed off onto your hair. Your hairs all became charged the same way with electrons. And when objects have the same charge, they **repel**. The result is a funny, stick-up-everywhere hairdo as your hairs try to get as far away from each other as possible!

DID YOU KNOW?

More static electricity builds up on dry days. When the air is humid, or full of moisture, the moisture in the air coats the surface of objects and makes it harder for an electrical charge to build up. Electricity can travel through water particles. But if it's very dry out, the electricity has nowhere to go and a static charge builds up.

When objects have opposite charges, they attract and move toward each other. Have you ever taken clothes made of different materials out of the dryer? Did they cling together? All that spinning causes some clothes to lose electrons and others to gain them. When you pull the two things apart, the electrons "jump" and you get a tiny spark and zap.

The same thing happens when you walk across a carpet with socks and then touch someone or a doorknob. Rubbing your feet against the carpet builds up static electricity. Then, when you touch something, that energy travels out your fingers and you get a quick, tiny zap!

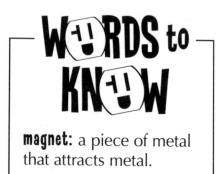

WORDS to KNOW

magnet: a piece of metal that attracts metal.

Experiments with Electricity

A few hundred years ago, scientists began studying and experimenting with static electricity. One of these people was William Gilbert (1544–1603). Gilbert was a doctor in England who studied the role of **magnets** in electricity. He invented a machine called a versorium. This machine had a wooden pointer that moved toward objects that had been electrically charged by rubbing them with wool or fur.

Later on, James Wimshurst (1832–1903) invented the Wimshurst Machine, which used turning glass **discs** to create a static electric charge. These charges were then stored in special containers called Leyden jars.

One of the most famous people to experiment with electricity was Benjamin Franklin (1706–1790). Franklin was a printer, writer, inventor, and Founding Father of America. Through his experiments, he helped prove that **lightning** and electricity were the same force. As the story goes, in 1752 Franklin went out in a thunderstorm and flew a kite with a key tied to the string. The kite's string became charged by the lightning and when Franklin touched the key, he got a shock. This proved to Franklin that lightning is electricity.

disc: a round, thin piece of material.

lightning: an electrical charge from a cloud.

Franklin certainly knew that attracting lightning from a cloud could kill him. So how did he protect himself? Some say he tied a silk ribbon to the end of his kite string. Silk is an insulator, so electricity from lightning moving down the string would have stopped when it hit the ribbon. But this was a very, very risky thing to do. You should never try this dangerous experiment yourself!

Lightning

Lightning is one of the most powerful and beautiful examples of static electricity. When there's a storm, wind moves around the clouds, which are made up of water droplets. Most lightning happens when clouds build up a negative charge on the bottom.

When the charge gets too great, a cloud tries to get rid of some of it.

The ground is positively charged because the negative charge of the cloud forces the negative charges in the ground away from the surface. So as the negative charge

expand: to spread out and take up more space.

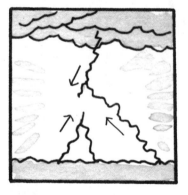

from the cloud moves down, the opposite positive charge from the ground or tall objects, like buildings and trees, moves up. The two meet in the middle and lightning strikes! But all of this happens so fast that our brains think the lightning is only moving downward.

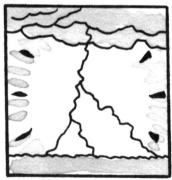

All that movement causes a lot of heat. Lightning is very hot, around 50,000 degrees Fahrenheit (27,000 degrees Celsius). That's about five times hotter than the sun. The heat causes the air to **expand** quickly. That rapid expansion of air causes a noise. What's the noise? Thunder!

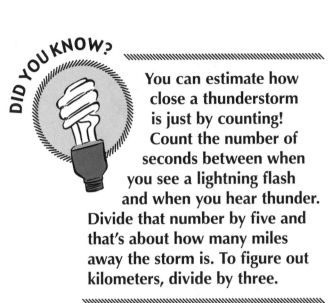

You can estimate how close a thunderstorm is just by counting! Count the number of seconds between when you see a lightning flash and when you hear thunder. Divide that number by five and that's about how many miles away the storm is. To figure out kilometers, divide by three.

Most of the time, lightning doesn't reach the ground. It just moves from cloud to cloud. These are called cloud flashes. But when lightning does reach the ground, the consequences can be deadly. Every year, lightning kills about 70 people in the United States. And many houses and buildings are hit and catch fire.

Keep Safe Around Lightning

Lightning storms can be very dangerous. Here are some ways to keep yourself safe.

* If you can hear thunder, head inside. Lightning can strike from 10 miles away (16 kilometers).

* If you're outside in a storm and the hairs on your arm stick up, find shelter immediately. It may mean the ground is building up a positive charge and you're a part of that positive charge.

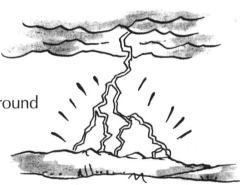

* Don't take shelter under a tree. Trees are usually the tallest thing around. They give lightning the easiest path to the ground so they attract lightning.

DID YOU KNOW?

The part of the lightning that comes down from the clouds is called a stepped leader. The part that reaches up from the ground is called a streamer.

WORDS to KNOW

lightning rod: a rod or pole used to move lightning's electrical charge safely into the ground.

resistance: a force that slows down another force.

Lightning always looks for the easiest path to travel. Tall objects give that easy path. Most tall buildings have a pointed metal rod or pole attached to the roof as protection from a lightning strike. These are called **lightning rods** and Benjamin Franklin invented them.

The rod connects to a huge piece of copper or aluminum wire. The lightning rod works because copper and aluminum are good conductors of electricity. So the tall rod provides an easy path for the huge electrical currents from lightning to travel to the ground and safely away from the building.

It's a Myth

Have you ever heard the saying, "Lightning never strikes the same place twice?" Well, it's not true! Lightning looks for the quickest path to the ground, the path of lowest **resistance**. A tall, often wet, object is less resistant to lightning than the air. So tall buildings can and often do get hit over and over. For example, the Empire State Building in New York is hit by lightning about 100 times a year. It remains undamaged because it is equipped with lightning rods.

Static Electricity

It's easier to build up static electricity on a cool, dry day. Here's an experiment that demonstrates this.

1 Go into the bathroom on a day when no one has taken a shower yet and the shower is dry.

2 Blow up the balloon until it's about 6 inches across (15 centimeters) and tie it off.

3 Rub one side of the balloon on your head or the wool blanket for 30 seconds. Use the stopwatch to time it.

4 Place the balloon against the wall, pull your hand away, and start the stopwatch again. Does the balloon stick? What do you know that would explain why this is happening? Predict how long you think the balloon will stay on the wall. Continue timing until the balloon falls. Record your results.

5 Now close the bathroom door and run a hot shower for 5 minutes. Make sure you have permission to do this first.

6 Rub the balloon on your head or the blanket for 30 seconds and place it on the wall of the bathroom like you did before. Observe what happens. Does the balloon still stick? Write down what you see in your journal.

WHAT'S HAPPENING? A hot shower creates steam, or humidity. This moisture builds up on the surface of the balloon. Since water allows electricity to move around more freely, the static electric charge flows away from the balloon instead of building up on it.

- bathroom with a shower
- balloon
- dry, clean hair or a wool blanket
- stopwatch
- science journal
- pencil

Electricity in Action

The ancient Greeks didn't understand static electricity, but they could see it. You can see it too with a few easy-to-find items.

1 Tie the string around the middle of one of the straws. Tape the string to the edge of a table so the straw hangs horizontally.

2 Rub the straw all over with the paper towel. Make sure to keep the straw in a horizontal position.

3 Rub the second straw with the paper towel. Slowly bring the side of the second straw toward the hanging straw. What happens and why? Create a scientific method worksheet in your journal and write your ideas down.

4 Predict what will happen if you move the paper towel toward the hanging straw. Now try it. What happens? Record your observations in your journal.

WHAT'S HAPPENING? When you rub the straws with the towel, you give them the same charge. Then when you put the straws close to each other, they repel. The paper towel has an opposite charge so the hanging straw is attracted to it.

> ⊱ 6-inch piece of string (15 centimeters)
> ⊱ 2 identical plastic straws
> ⊱ tape
> ⊱ table or cabinet
> ⊱ paper towel
> ⊱ science journal
> ⊱ pencil

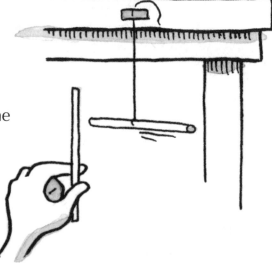

Electricity in Action—Again!

Is static electricity strong enough to move water? Create a scientific method worksheet. Make a prediction and write it down in your journal.

1 Turn the faucet on so there is a small but steady stream of water.

2 Next, use the paper towel to rub the straw. Count to 20 slowly while you do it.

3 Now, slowly bring the side of the straw toward the water. Look carefully. What's happening? Write or draw what you see. The water should be bending slightly! What does this tell you about how the straw and water are charged?

Stop the Zaps!

Static electricity can give people tiny shocks. You may not be able to avoid those zaps all the time, but here are a few simple ways you can cut back on the number of times they happen.

* Wear shoes inside your house. Rubbing socks against carpet can build up a static electric charge.

* Don't wear wool. Wool is a very good conductor of electricity.

* Ask your parents about running a humidifier in your house in the winter. More static electricity builds up in dry air. A humidifier is a device that puts moisture into the air.

Electroscope

William Gilbert used a device called a versorium to test an object's charge. You can make a similar device to see static electricity at work.

1 Flip the jar over onto the cardboard. Use your pencil to trace around the top. Cut the circle out. This will be your jar's lid.

2 Open up and straighten the paperclip until it looks like the letter L.

3 Carefully poke the paperclip into the lid and slide it through until about 1½ inches (3½ centimeters) of the top of the L is above the lid. The part with the right angle will be on the bottom.

4 Use a small piece of modeling clay on top of the lid to keep the wire in place.

5 Crumble a piece of aluminum foil into a ball that's a little bit smaller than a golf ball. Push it onto the wire that's above the lid. Be careful not to let the ball touch the cardboard.

6 Cut a piece of foil that is 3½ by ½ inches (about 9 by 1 centimeters). Fold it in half and drape it over the bent part of the wire so that it hangs below the lid. Use a small drop of glue under the fold to hold the foil in place.

- medium glass jar
- cardboard
- pencil
- scissors
- large, metal paperclip
- modeling clay
- aluminum foil
- ruler
- white glue
- tape
- balloon
- wool blanket
- science journal

7 Carefully place the lid on the jar. The foil flaps should be inside the jar. The foil ball should be on the outside. Use tape to attach the lid to the jar.

8 Now you're ready to try out your electroscope! Blow up the balloon and rub it on the wool blanket for about 30 seconds. Hold the balloon close to the foil ball. What happens to the foil flaps inside the jar?

9 Create a scientific method worksheet with a list of other things in your house that might have an electric charge. Test them out with your electroscope. Record you data in a chart like the one below. List the item in the first column and then check the appropriate box.

WHAT'S HAPPENING? The aluminum flaps should move apart. This is because the static electricity is moving from the balloon into the foil ball, down the wire, and into the foil flaps. The flaps have the same charge, so they are trying to move away from each other.

ITEM	CHARGE	NO CHARGE

Currents

With static electricity, electrons build up and stay where
they are until they touch another object and jump over.
But what if electrons are moving? Electrons in constant
motion create an electric current. It's kind of like water
flowing from a faucet to the end of a garden hose when
you turn the spigot. Electricity moves from one point to
another. Instead of going through a hose, electricity travels
along materials that are good conductors, like wires.

Conductors and Insulators

Electricity always takes the easiest path. Some materials allow an electric current to move through them easily. These are called conductors. Metals like silver, gold, copper, aluminum, brass, iron, and steel are all excellent conductors. So are people, animals, and water.

DID YOU KNOW?

Because water is an excellent conductor of electricity, you need to always keep electrical items away from water! And never go near water during a lightning storm.

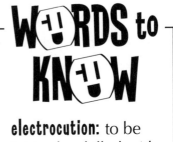

WORDS to KNOW

electrocution: to be injured or killed with electricity.

Other materials don't allow electricity to move through them easily. These are called insulators. Good insulators include things like glass, rubber, plastic, diamonds, and air. Insulators protect us from **electrocution**.

Look at the cord on any appliance in your house—an iron, a toaster, a coffee maker. You'll see a plastic covering on the outside. If you could look inside, you'd see a wire. Just DON'T cut the cord to look!

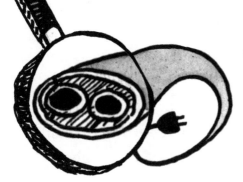

When you plug the cord into an outlet on the wall, an electric current moves along the wire into the appliance. The plastic covering on the cord makes it safe to handle anything that needs to be plugged in.

Birds on a Wire

Birds can stand on power lines and not get hurt. This is because electricity wants to move from a high charge to a low charge. Imagine the electrons are at a party and think, "It's too crowded here! I'm going to where it's less crowded." And the lowest-charged place around is the ground, not the bird. But what if the bird, or any living creature, touches a power line and something in contact with the ground at the same time? Then it becomes a pathway for the electricity.

DID YOU KNOW?

When some materials are cooled way down, they can carry electricity perfectly. They're called **superconductors.**

What about the people who work on power lines? Aren't they touching the ground? They are, but people who work on power lines are trained to work with electricity. They wear special boots and gloves and work out of buckets that are insulated. They also use special tools that protect them from the dangers of their job.

Just for Fun!

What did the man who stepped on a downed power line get?

A pair of "shocks!"

Keep Safe Around Power Lines

* You should assume all power lines are charged! Some lines are insulated but most of them are not. Touching a power line or even touching something that is touching a power line (like a kite or a ladder) can hurt or even kill you.

* Never climb trees near power lines or play near them.

* Never touch a wire that has fallen down.

* If you are riding in your car and come across a downed power line, stay in your car. The rubber tires are insulators that can help protect you.

Voltage, Amps, and Watts

Let's think about that garden hose again. When you turn on the spigot you usually don't have to wait for the water. It starts moving down the hose right away. That's because there is **pressure** on the water as it goes through the pipes to reach the hose. When the water valve is opened, swoosh! The pressure is released and water flows.

The flow of electricity works the same way. There's a force making electrons flow called **voltage**, or volts for short. A higher voltage means more pressure is building up. And this means more **potential** power.

WORDS to KNOW

pressure: the force that pushes on an object.

voltage (volts): the force that moves electrons in an electric current.

potential: something that is possible, or can develop into something real.

Batteries can supply this kind of force. Most batteries you handle only have about 1.5 volts. That's not very high potential to do work. That's why they don't hurt you. Batteries in use can get very warm, though, so still be careful.

A regular wall outlet has a lot more potential power than a 1.5-volt battery. Its 120 volts is enough force to give you a powerful shock. That's why you should never touch an outlet.

WORDS to KNOW

battery: a device that produces an electric current using chemicals.

ampere (amp): the measurement of the amount of electric current.

wattage (watts): the amount of power that's created or used.

In an electric current, electrons move very quickly from atom to atom. The number of electrons that move past a point at a time is measured in units called **amperes**, or amps. Think of it like rivers flowing. A large river and a small river may travel at the same rate, but more water flows in a large river. A higher number of amps means more electricity is flowing.

DID YOU KNOW?

A wire carrying 1 amp has about 6,250,000,000,000,000,000 electrons flowing across per second!

Volts and amps together equal power to do work. The amount of power is called **wattage**, or watts. Watts measure how much energy is released per second. To figure out how much power is available, scientists use the formula amps x volts = watts.

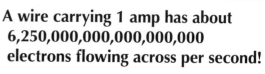

$$A \times V = W$$

Did a Frog Help Invent the Battery?

A teacher in Italy named Luigi Galvani (1737–1798) **dissected** frogs to study their bodies. One night, the scissors he was using touched the nerves in the frog's legs and the dead frog's legs moved! Nerves are special pathways between the body and the brain. Galvani thought the frog's legs moved because they had electricity running through them. He called this "animal electricity."

dissect: to cut something apart to study what is inside.

theory: an idea that could explain how or why something happens.

Another Italian teacher named Alessandro Volta (1745–1827) heard about this, but he had a different **theory**. He thought the frog's legs jumped because of the metal tools Galvani used.

Volta decided to test his idea. He began by stacking different metal discs on top of each other. But when he touched them, nothing happened. There was no charge. Then he soaked a piece of cardboard in salt water and put it between zinc and copper discs. These units, called cells, did produce a small charge.

Next, Volta stacked many cells on top of each other, each separated by a layer of cardboard soaked in salt water. When he touched the stack, he got a huge shock! *Zap!*

WORDS to KNOW

chemical reaction: an event that causes the atoms of one or more kinds of matter to rearrange.

molecule: a group of atoms bound together by sharing electrons.

electrode: a conductor through which electricity enters or leaves an object like a battery.

electrolyte: a liquid or paste in a battery that allows for the flow of electric current.

anode: the end of a battery marked with a - sign.

cathode: the end of a battery marked with a + sign.

ion: atoms or molecules with extra or missing electrons.

What was happening? A **chemical reaction** between **molecules** in the materials Volta used caused electrons to move. The salt water was a great conductor. This was the first simple battery.

A regular battery, like the kind you find in a flashlight today, works in a similar way. It has two metal plates called **electrodes** at the ends of the battery. An **electrolyte** connects the electrodes. The **anode** is the flat metal plate on one end. It is marked as the negative end. The **cathode** is marked as the positive end and always has a bump on it. The cathode and anode are made of different metals.

When a battery is hooked up, a chemical reaction starts inside. The electrolyte has something called **ions** that carry electrons from the cathode to the anode. This causes the anode to have more electrons. The electrons want to be in balance. So when a battery is hooked up to a circuit, the electrons head out of the anode, power the object using electricity, and then travel back to the cathode.

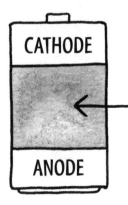

CATHODE **+**

ELECTROLYTE

ANODE **—**

Watts in Action

A watt is a unit of power. It measures the amount of power generated or the amount used by an electrical object. The higher the watts, the more power and the more work that can be done. Here's a simple way to see this in action.

1 Fill both balloons with water and tie them off.

2 Hold the small balloon above the sink. Carefully poke the bottom of it with the pin. Observe how fast the water comes out.

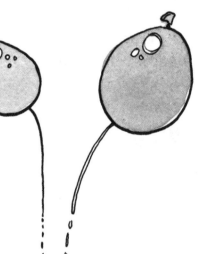

3 Now hold the bigger balloon over the sink. Carefully poke the bottom of it with the pin. Observe how fast the water comes out.

4 Which balloon pushed out the water with more power? Why do you think that is?

DID YOU KNOW?

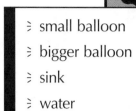

Look at the top or the base of a light bulb that's not screwed in. You'll see a number followed by a W. It might say, 60W, for example. That's the bulb's wattage, or the amount of energy used to make the bulb shine. Watts can also mean the amount of power an electrical device needs to run. Appliances have watt numbers on them to tell you that. A typical washing machine uses 500W and a dryer uses 4,000W!

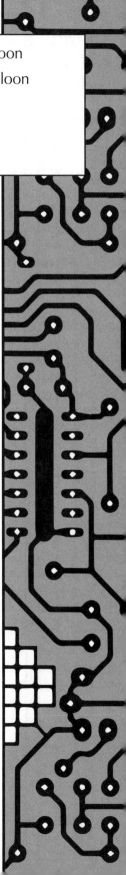

Voltaic Pile Model

Alessandro Volta created the first cell battery. Here's a way to make a model of his battery. The best part? You can eat it!

1 Lay a lid on a flat surface with the rim facing down. Place a cookie in the middle. Pretend the cookie is the face of a clock. Using the marker, make a mark on the lid just outside the cookie's edge at the "12 o'clock" point. Make marks at the "4 o'clock" and "8 o'clock" points, too.

2 Use the hole punch to make holes at the three marks. Mark and punch holes in the second lid the same way. You should have two matching lids.

3 Tightly wrap the pencils in aluminum foil. Place either one of the lids on a flat surface so the rim is facing down.

4 Gently push a pencil into each hole. You may have to wiggle the pencils a bit if the holes aren't quite big enough. The pencils should be pushed down enough so that they touch the flat surface.

SUPPLIES

- ⋛ 2 identical, small plastic lids, about 3 inches in diameter (7½ centimeters)
- ⋛ 10–12 vanilla-chocolate sandwich cookies
- ⋛ permanent marker
- ⋛ hole punch
- ⋛ 3 new pencils
- ⋛ aluminum foil

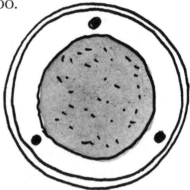

DID YOU KNOW?

The word voltage comes from Alessandro Volta. But you probably guessed that already, didn't you?

5 Stack the cookies in between the three pencils. The cookies represent cells. Remember, in Volta's battery, these cells were made of copper, zinc, and cardboard soaked in salt water.

6 Slide the second lid, rim facing down, onto the pencils.

7 Push the lid down until it touches the top of the cookies. Your model is ready!

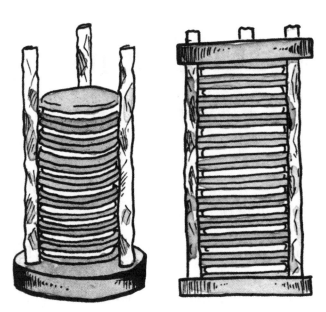

THINGS TO THINK ABOUT: You used plastic lids and aluminum-covered pencils. But Volta used a wood base and glass rods in his battery. Why do you think he used these materials?

Now, that's a big battery!

The world's biggest battery was turned on in 2012 in China. It's housed in a building the size of a football field and can store 32 megawatt-hours of energy. A megawatt is equal to 1,000,000 watts! The battery, which is hooked into a wind- and solar-power grid, can produce enough power for 12,000 homes and businesses during an electrical shortage or outage.

Conductors and Insulators

Make a circuit and try out different objects you have at home to discover whether they are conductors or insulators. You can find the LED light needed for this experiment at an **electronics** supply store or a hobby shop.

CAUTION: Have an adult strip the wires for you.

1 Cut the wire into three pieces, 10 inches (25 centimeters), 8 inches (20 centimeters), and 7 inches long (18 centimeters).

2 Ask an adult to strip 1 inch of insulation off each end of each of the copper wires (2½ centimeters).

3 Tape the two batteries together end-to-end with electrical tape to make one long battery with a positive end and a negative end.

4 Look at your LED. It should have two wires (or leads) coming down from the bottom. One of these is the positive end and the other is the negative end. Positive leads are usually longer. If you happen to have an LED with legs of the same length, look inside the bottom of the bulb for two metal triangular pieces. The smaller one connects to the positive lead and the bigger one connects to the negative lead.

Supplies

- 25 inches insulated copper wire (63 centimeters)
- scissors
- 2 D batteries
- electrical tape
- 10 mm LED light (rated for 3.5 volts)
- various items to test, such as a paperclip, pencil, straw, and penny
- science journal
- pencil

WORDS to KNOW

electronics: devices that use computer parts to control the flow of electricity.

POSITIVE LEAD   NEGATIVE LEAD

5 Tape one end of the middle-sized piece of wire to the positive end of the battery. Wrap the other end around the positive lead of the LED. You can use a small bit of tape to make sure they stay together.

6 Wrap one end of the shortest wire to the negative lead of the LED and use tape to make sure they stay together.

7 Next, tape one end of the longest piece of wire to the negative end of the D battery. Now you've created an open circuit. You should have two open wires.

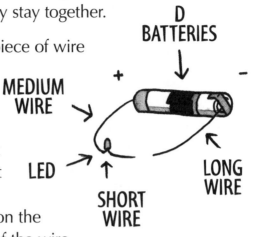

D BATTERIES

MEDIUM WIRE

LED

SHORT WIRE

LONG WIRE

8 Start a scientific method worksheet in your science journal. Copy the chart below into your journal to record your data. Place the items you want to test on the table, in between the two open ends of the wire. Which items do you think are conductors and which are insulators?

9 Hold each wire and touch the sides of the items one at a time. Does the light bulb light up? Record your observations. Try to notice which items are the best conductors and note it in your journal.

WHAT'S HAPPENING? When you place a conductor in between the two wires, the light bulb lights up. This is because the item is completing (or closing) the circuit. If you put an insulator in between the wires, the circuit remains open. The electricity can't move and won't light the bulb.

ITEM	INSULATOR	CONDUCTOR

Lemon Battery

This battery won't have enough charge to light a bulb, but you'll be able to feel a slight electric current.

1 Roll the lemon around on a table or in your hands until it's soft and juicy.

2 Next, unfold the paperclip so it has a straight end and an end with a hook. Wash and dry the paperclip.

3 Carefully push the straight end of the paperclip into the top of the lemon so the loop sticks up.

4 Fold the copper wire in half and twist the ends together. Leave a small loop at the top. It should look kind of like a needle. Wash and dry the wire piece.

5 Carefully poke the end of the copper wire into the lemon about half an inch away from the paperclip (1½ centimeters). Make sure they aren't touching.

6 Use the top of your tongue to touch the tops of both the paperclip and copper wire at the same time. Do you feel a tingle or have a funny taste in your mouth?

WHAT'S HAPPENING? The different metals in the paperclip and the copper wire create an electric charge that can flow through the liquid acid in the lemon. Your wet tongue completes the circuit!

> * large lemon
> * large paperclip
> * 4-inch uninsulated copper wire (10 centimeters)
> * soap, water, and paper towel

PAPER CLIP

COPPER WIRE

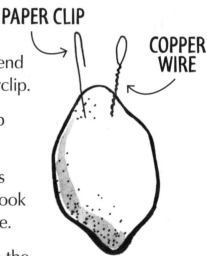

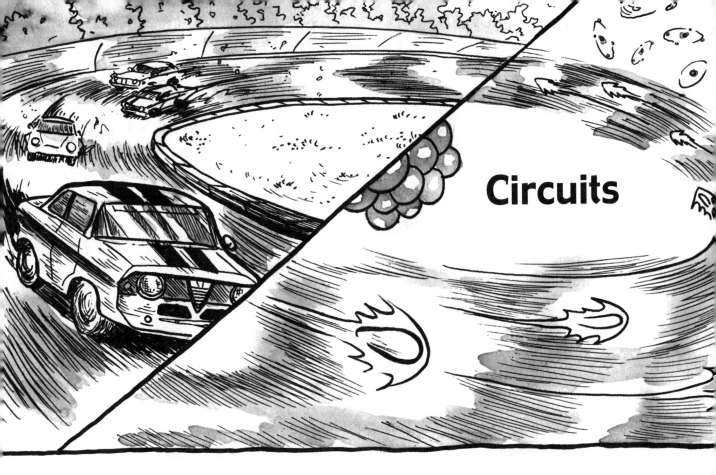

Circuits

Imagine a racetrack. The cars are revving up at the starting line and someone waves the flag. They're off! As the cars speed around the track, nothing gets in their way. They keep going around and around until someone waves the flag to signal the end of the race.

- -

A traveling path that begins and ends at the same spot is called a circuit. Racetracks are circuits. Electricity travels in a path we call an **electrical circuit**. In the simplest circuit, electricity moves from a power source through a conductor to an electrical device and then back to the power source. In this kind of circuit, electricity is always flowing and the device is always on. But what if we want to turn that flow of electricity off?

Most circuits have built-in breaks that we can control to stop the flow of electricity. These breaks are called **switches**. They open and close a circuit.

We use switches all the time to turn things on and off. Just like the cars on a racetrack, electricity needs a clear path. If there's nothing stopping the electrons, the circuit is closed and electricity is flowing. If there's a break in the path, the circuit is open and electrons can't flow through.

WORDS to KNOW

electrical circuit: the pathway electricity follows.

switch: a control that opens or closes a circuit.

load: the object that uses the electricity in a circuit.

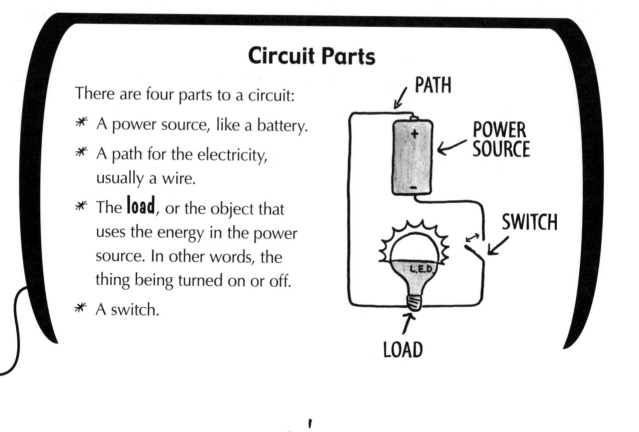

Circuit Parts

There are four parts to a circuit:

* A power source, like a battery.
* A path for the electricity, usually a wire.
* The **load**, or the object that uses the energy in the power source. In other words, the thing being turned on or off.
* A switch.

PATH

POWER SOURCE

SWITCH

L.E.D.

LOAD

In a **series circuit**, there is only one path along which electricity can travel. The electricity goes from one load to another, to another, and so on. Think of an old string of Christmas tree lights. All the lights rely on the same power source, so if one bulb goes out the rest do too. This is because the burned-out bulb opens the circuit.

WORDS to KNOW

series circuit: a circuit with a single path from the power source to the load and back to the power source.

parallel circuit: a circuit with a pathway to the power source for each load.

In a **parallel circuit**, each load has its own pathway back to the power source. These types of circuits are helpful when we need things to stay on when another load is out. Think of a hallway in your house with two or more lights that turn on and off with the same switch.

If one goes out, the rest keep working so you can still find your way around. A lot of new strings of Christmas lights work this way today.

DID YOU KNOW?

A 747 airplane has over 100 miles of wires connecting its circuits (161 kilometers).

The Light Bulb

Maybe you've heard that Thomas Edison (1847–1931) invented the light bulb. He wasn't actually the first, but all the bulbs before his burned out after a few minutes. In earlier bulbs, the metal thread the electricity ran through, called the **filament**, got too hot and burned up quickly. It was also very expensive.

In 1879, Edison used cotton thread for the filament, which didn't cost as much. He also decided to take out more of the oxygen from inside the glass bulb. Without oxygen, fire can't burn. So less oxygen meant less chance of the filament burning. His bulb lasted at least 13 hours! By 1925, half of all homes in the United States had electric power. The rest still used gas light and candles.

filament: the wire used as the conducting material inside a light bulb.

incandescent: a source of electric light that works by heating a filament.

Today, we have different kinds of light bulbs. Traditional **incandescent** bulbs now use a filament made of a metal called tungsten. Tungsten doesn't melt until it reaches 6,191 degrees Fahrenheit (3,422 degrees Celsius)! Each piece of tungsten is about 20 inches long (50 centimeters), but it's coiled up tightly so it takes up less space.

TUNGSTEN FILAMENT

SUPPORT WIRES

GLASS MOUNT

BULB

THREAD CONTACT

FOOT CONTACT

Compact fluorescent lights (CFLs) use much less energy to give off the same amount of light as incandescent bulbs. And they last a lot longer. CFLs have no filament at all. Instead, they have spiral-shaped tubes that hold gases, including mercury. The inside of the tubes is coated with a white powder called phosphor. When electricity runs through the bulb, the mercury heats up. It gives off a special kind of light called **ultraviolet light**, which causes the phosphor to glow brightly.

SPIRAL TUBING

PHOSPHOR COATING

GASES (ARGON AND MERCURY)

BASE

WORDS to KNOW

compact fluorescent light: a light bulb that uses less electricity and lasts longer than an incandescent light bulb.

ultraviolet light: a kind of light with short wavelengths. It can't be seen with the naked eye.

greenhouse gases: gases that trap heat in the atmosphere and make the planet warm.

atmosphere: the blanket of air surrounding the earth.

DID YOU KNOW?

What if every American home replaced just one incandescent light bulb with a CFL? It would save enough energy to light more than 3 million homes for a year and cut more than $600 million in energy costs each year. It would also prevent the release of **greenhouse gases** into the **atmosphere** equal to more than 800,000 cars.

Another type of energy-efficient light is called an LED. These last 100 times longer than incandescent bulbs and use one-fourth the energy. They even last 10 times longer than CFLs. LED stands for "light-emitting **diode**." A diode is a **semiconductor** that conducts an electric current, but only partly. It lets electricity flow in one direction, but if it tries to flow the other way, it can't get through.

WORDS to KNOW

diode: an electronic part that limits the flow of current to one direction.

semiconductor: a material that can be controlled to sometimes, but not always, conduct electricity.

direct current (DC): an electric current where electricity flows one direction.

DID YOU KNOW?

LEDs come in lots of colors like red, yellow, and blue. They're inside glow sticks, toy light sabers, and light-up jewelry.

But LED bulbs are expensive and the light they give out can look dimmer than light from other bulbs. Also, they start to dim once they've been on for a while.

AC and DC

Electricity can travel in different ways. If it moves in only one direction in a circuit we say it's a **direct current**, or DC. Batteries produce direct current. We use DC in things like cellphones, flashlights, and laptop computers when they aren't plugged in. The electricity flows from the positive end of the battery to the negative end of the battery through a conductor until we turn the device off using a switch.

DIRECT CURRENT

In other circuits, electrons vibrate back and forth and change direction. We call this **alternating current**, or AC. When electricity has to travel over long distances, AC is used more than DC. Most electrical power coming from a wall outlet into our homes and offices is an alternating current.

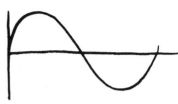

ALTERNATING CURRENT

How Does Electricity Make it to Our Houses?

Have you ever wondered how electricity gets to your house in the first place? To supply large areas with electricity, we use a system of **power plants** called a **power grid**. You can think of this grid as one giant circuit. These grids connect to other grids across the country and sometimes across continents.

Just for Fun!

Why did the gardner switch from seeds to light bulbs?

To grow a power plant.

WORDS to KNOW

alternating current (AC): an electric current where electricity flows back and forth.

power plant: a place where electrical power is produced to be spread out and used.

power grid: a system of power plants and circuits.

Circuit Symbols

People who work with electricity use special symbols to draw circuits. These are called schematic symbols. Here are a few common ones.

RESISTOR

TWO CELL BATTERY

LAMP

OPEN SWITCH

CLOSED SWITCH

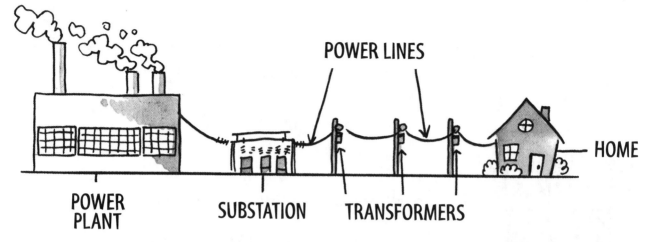

POWER LINES

HOME

POWER
PLANT

SUBSTATION

TRANSFORMERS

A grid works like this: first, power plants make electricity using different methods. We'll learn about these methods in later chapters. Next, the electricity is sent out along power lines to smaller power plants, called substations. From the substations the electricity goes into **transformers**. A transformer is a device that either raises or lowers the voltage of the electricity. Raising the voltage helps push the electricity along the grid.

W◖◗RDS to KN◗◖W

transformer: something that increases or decreases the voltage of an alternating current.

breaker panel: the electrical box that sends electric power entering a house to each plug and switch.

The electricity keeps moving along in this way. Finally it reaches a transformer that lowers it to a voltage that is safe to use at home.

The electricity goes into your house through a special box called a **breaker panel**. Ask you parents to show you the breaker panel in your house. From the breaker panel, electrical wires run throughout your house and into outlets.

> ⋛ adult
> ⋛ breaker panel
> ⋛ science journal
> ⋛ pencil
> ⋛ friend to help (optional)
> ⋛ cellphones or walk-talkies (optional)

Breaker Box Test

It is important to know which switches control the power in different areas of you house. If you lose power in a room, you can check to see if the switch is off. The breaker panel is where electricity comes into your house.

CAUTION: Always have an adult with you when you check it out.

1 Go to the breaker panel where you live. Open the panel door and take a look. It won't hurt you—the electricity is insulated. Draw what you see in your journal. You'll see a bunch of small switches that are labeled with rooms or appliances. These identify the circuits in your house or building.

2 Ask permission to flip a switch. Go to the room and see what happens. You can also use cellphones or walkie-talkies to ask a friend in the room to tell you what happens.

3 Record your observations. If everything goes off, you'll know all the outlets in a room are on the same circuit.

4 When you're done, be sure to flip the breaker switch back on and close the breaker panel door.

DID YOU KNOW?

Wires that carry electricity can lose their insulation. If this happens and the wires are too close to one another, the electrons can jump from one to the other. This is called a short circuit. Short circuits can cause power outages and fires. This is why you should never use a cord that has exposed wires.

Simple Circuit

⋛ light bulb from a
   flashlight
⋛ 2 D batteries
⋛ aluminum foil
⋛ electrical tape
⋛ science journal
⋛ pencil

You can create your own simple circuit to light a bulb. Ask permission from an adult before you remove the light bulb from the flashlight.

1 Cut two pieces of aluminum foil, each about 12 by 2 inches (30 by 5 centimeters). Fold and pinch each into a long, skinny, ribbon-like strip. Tape an end of one of the aluminum strips to the positive end of one battery. Use electrical tape.

2 Tape an end of the second aluminum strip to the negative end of the same battery. Tape the other end of this aluminum strip to the ring of metal at the bottom of the bulb.

3 On the very bottom of the light bulb there should be a tiny metal base. You are going to touch the loose end of the first aluminum strip to the base of the light bulb. But be very careful that it doesn't touch the second aluminum strip. You can either hold the first aluminum strip in place or tape it in place.

4 What happens to the light bulb? Does it glow? Is it dim or bright? Write what you observe in your journal. What do you think will happen if you add the second battery to the circuit? Write down your prediction.

5 Now tape the second battery to the first one. The positive end must be touching the negative end of the second battery. Tape the piece of aluminum that was on the negative end of the first battery to the negative end of the second battery. What happens? Why do you think that's happening? Write down your ideas and observations in your journal.

Paperclip Switch

⋛ your simple circuit

⋛ scissors

⋛ paperclip

⋛ piece of thick cardboard, 2 by 3 inches (5 by 7½ centimeters)

⋛ 2 pushpins

⋛ science journal

⋛ pencil

Switches allow you to control the flow of electricity. Think about how often you flip a switch to turn something on or off.

1 Cut through one of the foil strips from your simple circuit, halfway between the battery and the bulb. Open the paperclip, leaving a loop at each end.

2 Place one end of the cut foil strip on the cardboard. Stick a pushpin through one of the paperclip loops, through the foil and into the cardboard. Some of the metal should be showing and the paperclip should be able to move.

3 Now, using the other pushpin, attach the other foil strip to the other end of the cardboard. It should be close enough so that paperclip reaches, but don't put the pushpin through the second paperclip loop. The paperclip should to be able to swing between the two pushpins.

Just for Fun!

Why did the electric current start going the other way?

It wanted to "switch" things up!

4 Now try your switch! Swing the paperclip to touch the metal part of the second pushpin. Is your light glowing? If not, make sure the foil strips haven't come loose from the light or battery.

THINGS TO THINK ABOUT: Can you think of other materials that might work instead of the paperclip? Use a scientific method worksheet to organize your experiment. Then try them out and see if they do.

Nightlight

You can turn your nightlight on and off with the switch you make! Buy the LED light needed for this project at a craft store or where electronic parts are sold.

- scissors
- ruler
- cardboard tube
- electrical tape
- markers, stickers for decorating
- aluminum foil
- 2 D batteries
- 10 millimeter LED light (rated for 3.5 volts)

1 Cut your cardboard tube so it's 4½ inches high (11 centimeters). You can tape two empty toilet paper rolls together and cut them to the right height, too. Use electrical tape to cover one opened end of the tube. Decorate the tube as you'd like.

2 Fold and pinch the aluminum foil into a skinny, ribbon-like piece that is 6¼ inches long (15½ centimeters).

3 Stack the batteries one on top of the other. Make sure the positive end of one is touching the negative end of the other. Use the electrical tape to tape them together. You should now have a long battery that is positive on the top and negative on the bottom.

4 Use a small piece of tape to secure one end of the aluminum strip to the negative end of the battery.

5 Holding the aluminum strip against the battery, carefully place the battery inside the cardboard tube. The negative end goes down. The strip should be sticking out a little bit from the top of the tube. Fold it over to make a small flap.

6 Look at your LED. It should have two wires (or leads) coming down from the bottom. One of these is the positive end and the other is the negative end. Positive leads are usually longer. If you happen to have an LED with legs of the same length, look inside the bottom of the bulb for two metal triangular pieces. The smaller one connects to the positive lead. The bigger one connects to the negative lead.

7 Make a small L-shaped bend at the bottom of the positive lead. Tape it flat to the top of your battery. You'll probably have to use a few pieces of tape to get it to stay in place.

8 Carefully make a small L-shaped bend at the bottom of the negative lead.

9 Now you're ready to light the bulb! To turn your light on, simply wrap the flap of aluminum foil around the L-shaped bend. Did your bulb light?

10 If your bulb didn't light up, check to see if your circuit is closed. Make sure the batteries are still stacked right on top of each other and that the LED lead hasn't shifted off the top of the battery.

WHAT'S HAPPENING? The flap of aluminum is acting as a switch. Can you think of another way to make a switch using a paperclip or another conductor? **Hint:** Look back to the results from your conductors and insulators experiment from earlier in this book to find other materials that are good conductors.

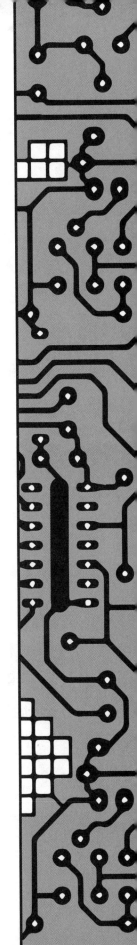

Electromagnetism

It's fun to play with magnets. You can make them pick things up or stick to their objects. And if you put two close together, sometimes they stick to each other and sometimes they push away from each other. Sounds a lot like objects with an electric charge, right? This is because of **magnetism**, a force that either attracts or repels materials that are like it. Electricity and magnetism are connected. Where you find one, you will always find the other.

One of the first people to discover this was Hans Christian Oersted (1777–1851). Oersted was a college professor from Denmark. One day, he was talking to his students about electricity when he accidently passed a wire with an electric current over a **compass**. When he did, the compass needle changed direction. Instead of pointing north, it pointed to the wire. It was following the flow of the electric current. This showed Oersted that the electricity in the wire had magnetism.

compass: an instrument that uses a magnetized needle to find north.

magnetic field: an invisible area (or field) created by a magnet.

Magnetic Fields

Like batteries, a magnet has two different ends. We say a battery has a positive and negative end. With a magnet, we say it has a north pole and a south pole. And just as with charged atoms, like poles repel each other and opposite poles attract. An invisible force flows in the space around the magnet. It goes from the north pole to the south pole and back again. This force doesn't just go everywhere. It stays in a certain area. This area is called a **magnetic field**.

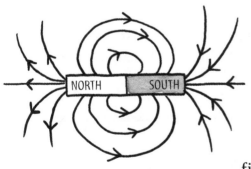

Any object with magnetism has a magnetic field. An object's magnetic field is strongest right around the object. It gets weaker as it moves away. You'll know your magnet is inside another magnet's magnetic field when you feel a push or pull.

Oersted's discovery that an electric current creates a magnetic field was important. A few years later, a British scientist named Michael Faraday (1791–1867) showed that a moving magnetic field creates an electric current. He pushed a magnetic rod back and forth through a bundle of wire. It turned out that when the rod wasn't moving, there wasn't a charge. But when the rod was moving, there was an electrical charge. This is because the magnetic field was actually moving the electrons in the wire. And electrons in motion mean one thing—electricity!

physicist: someone who studies energy and matter.

electromagnetism: magnetism created by a current of electricity.

DID YOU KNOW?

Michael Faraday is often called the "Father of Electricity." Along with showing that a moving magnetic field could create electricity, he discovered that electrical charges put out "waves." We use these waves to send sounds over the radio.

A Scottish **physicist** named James Clerk Maxwell (1831–1879) combined the discoveries of Oersted, Faraday, and others into one theory called **electromagnetism**. It says that electricity and magnetism are two parts of the same force. Electromagnetism is the magnetic force created by a current of electricity.

Super Magnets: Electromagnets

The magnets you use to stick things on your refrigerator or to pick up small metal objects are called permanent magnets. That means they keep their magnetism all the time. But by using electricity, we can make magnets that turn on and off. These magnets are called **electromagnets**.

electromagnet: a powerful magnet whose magnetism is turned on and off using electricity.

Electromagnets are made by first wrapping an insulated wire around an iron rod. Then, an electrical current is sent through the wire. What happens? A magnetic field forms around the iron rod, and the rod becomes magnetic. Once the current is turned off, the rod stops being magnetic.

Electromagnets are all around you in things you use every day like car locks, doorbells, telephones, and refrigerators. We can control the power of an electromagnet. A huge iron rod with a lot of wire wrapped around it makes a really strong magnet. The more wire, the stronger the magnetism. Junkyards use large electromagnets to lift and move heavy objects like cars and scrap metal. Some roller coasters use them to hold and stop cars along the track.

Hey! Earth Has a North and South Pole, too!

Magnets have a north and a south end. Does this sound familiar? The earth also has a North Pole and a South Pole. That's because Earth is kind of like a giant magnet. You can't see it, but our planet has a magnetic field all around it. The northernmost point of this magnetic field is the North Pole. The southernmost point of the magnetic field is the South Pole. The poles do not stay in one place. They move around a little bit each day.

A compass will always point toward the North Pole. This can be useful if you're lost. If you can find north, you can find other directions, too. Compasses use a needle that has been magnetized. The needle can spin freely. One end is usually marked in red or with an "N." Because the needle is magnetized, it lines up with Earth's magnetic field. The needle shows which direction is north.

Magnet Warnings

Magnets can damage computers. They can damage other things like video tapes and credit cards, too. Always keep magnets away from these things. Magnets can also hurt you if you swallow them. Never put them in your mouth. Keep them away from your younger brothers and sisters, too.

Magnetic Field Art

What happens when a magnet gets close to lots of tiny pieces of iron? Does the magnet's magnetic field tell them where to go? You can find iron filings at science supply stores or in the science or educational aisle of many toy stores. They are also available online.

1 Lay the magnet on a flat surface. Have your friend hold the piece of card stock flat over the magnet about 3 inches away (7½ centimeters).

2 Hold the bottle of iron filings above the paper. Sprinkle them onto the paper. Make sure the iron filings are evenly distributed.

3 What do you see? Make a drawing of it in your science journal. When you're done, be sure to pour your iron filings back into the bottle. Just don't let them touch the magnet. Otherwise, they'll stick and it will be hard to get them all off. Of course you can play around with it if you don't mind the mess and you want to have some fun!

THINGS TO THINK ABOUT: What do you notice happens to the filings around the magnet's poles? Did the filings make a straight or a curved line? What do you think would happen to the filings if you try a magnet of a different shape? What would its magnetic field look like? Experiment and find out!

SUPPLIES
- bar magnet
- friend to help
- piece of card stock
- bottle of iron filings
- science journal
- pencil

Make a Compass Move

Are you ready to see a magnetic field in action?

1 Set your compass on a flat surface. The needle will settle to point north.

2 Now, slowly bring the magnet toward the compass from the side. What happens to the compass needle? Does it move or jump? Draw or write what you see in your journal.

THINGS TO THINK ABOUT: Do you think the size of the magnet affects how much the needle moves? Why or why not? Experiment with a bigger magnet and find out.

Roller Coaster Magnetism

Magnets are used in all kinds of machines. They are even used in roller coasters. Very strong magnets repel, which can launch cars so quickly they can reach speeds of 100 miles per hour in just seconds (161 kilometers per hour).

Magnets are used to slow down or stop roller coasters, too. The first coaster to use a magnetic braking system was the Millennium Force at Cedar Point in Sandusky, Ohio. It was built in 2000. Today, many roller coasters use magnets to brake because they don't need replacing very often and they save electricity.

Compass

Compasses were invented in ancient China. They were first used as part of fortune telling. It wasn't until much later that people saw how useful a compass could be to help them find their way around. You can't take this compass on a hike, but you can use it at home.

⋛ glass or aluminum dish

⋛ water

⋛ plastic lid off a milk jug

⋛ sewing needle

⋛ bar magnet marked with a north and south end

1 Fill the dish with about 2 inches of water (5 centimeters).

2 Place the lid in the water. It doesn't matter if it's face up or down, as long as it's floating.

3 Rub the north end of the magnet along the whole length of the needle. Move from the eye of the needle to the sharp pointy end and only go in one direction. (Don't rub it back and forth or it won't work!) Rub the needle about 20 times to magnetize the needle.

4 Carefully lay the needle on top of the floating lid. What happens? The tip of the needle should slowly move to point north.

THINGS TO THINK ABOUT: Using your compass, can you figure out which way south, east, and west are? Examine a few compasses up close. Some use liquid. Some do not. What other differences can you notice on other compasses?

Just for Fun!

What did the big brother magnet say to his little brother?

"Stick with me, kid!"

Electromagnet

For this project, you will need a screwdriver that is not magnetized. To test this, try picking up a paperclip or nail with the tip of the screwdriver before you begin.

CAUTION: Never strip an electrical wire yourself. Ask an adult to do it for you. Be careful once your electromagnet is on, because it will get hot. Don't forget to turn it off when you're done.

> ⋛ non-magnetized screwdriver
> ⋛ 48 to 54 inches of insulated copper wire (121 to 137 centimeters)
> ⋛ scissors
> ⋛ electrical tape
> ⋛ 2 D batteries
> ⋛ paperclips

1 Wrap the wire tightly around the metal part of the screwdriver in a spiral. Make as many loops around the screwdriver as you can without overlapping them. The more loops your electromagnet has, the more power it will have. Leave 2 inches of the screwdriver uncovered (5 centimeters) and leave about 5 inches of loose wire on the ends (12 centimeters). You can use a little bit of electrical tape to keep the coiled wire in place.

2 Ask an adult to use the scissors to carefully strip off about 1 inch of insulation at each end of the wire (2½ centimeters).

3 Stack the batteries with the positive end of one touching the negative end of the other. Wrap the middle with electrical tape. You should now have a long battery with a positive end and a negative end.

4 Next, tape one end of the stripped wire to the positive side of the battery and the other end of the stripped wire to the negative end of the battery.

56

5 Your electromagnet is on. Hold the screwdriver by the handle. See if you can pick up the paperclips. Be careful! The longer you use your electromagnet, the hotter your wires and battery will become.

THINGS TO THINK ABOUT:

How many paperclips do you think your electromagnet can pick up? Make a prediction and test it. Do you think you could pick up something bigger than a paperclip? Give it a try!

Maglev Trains

Maglev trains (short for magnetic levitation trains) use strong magnetic fields to hover over the tracks. Because the trains aren't touching anything, there's no rolling resistance. This means they can go very fast, over 300 miles per hour (482 kilometers)!

Scientists in China are working on a maglev train that runs inside a vacuum tunnel. This would get rid of air resistance. These trains would go around 745 miles per hour (1,200 kilometers per hour), faster than passenger airplanes!

Motors and Generators

What do fans, refrigerators, electric pencil sharpeners, and remote-control toys have in common? They all have motors. Electric motors are machines that change electrical power into motion. This kind of motion, like spinning the blades of a fan, is called **mechanical** power. And guess what? All electric motors, big and small, use magnets to create motion.

- -

If you could take apart an electric motor, you'd see magnets inside. Some are permanent magnets and some are electromagnets. In a small motor, there are two permanent magnets with opposite poles facing each other. There's something invisible but strong between those poles—a magnetic field.

WORDS to KNOW

mechanical: relating to machines or tools.

armature: the spinning part of a motor, made of tightly coiled wires.

axle: a rod on which something spins.

winding: wire wrapped around an armature.

The spinning part of the motor is called the **armature**. It sits inside the magnetic field. The armature is an electromagnet. It's made of a wire coiled tightly around a metal **axle**. An axle is a rod that spins, or rolls. It's what turns the tires on a bike, makes the wheels turn on a remote control car, and spins the blades that sharpen a pencil. In other words, it makes things move!

Go, Motor, Go!

Left alone, the armature does nothing. But when an electric current passes through the **windings** of the coil, the axle becomes a magnet. It has a north pole and a south pole. So what happens? The coil turns to find its opposite charge on the permanent magnet. But we don't want the spinning to just stop there. That wouldn't produce much motion.

To keep the electric current flowing, it needs to be changing direction. On a permanent magnet, the poles are always in the same place. But on an electromagnet, we can flip-flop the poles by changing the flow of the

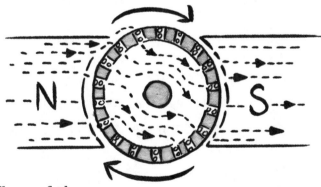

electric current. This means the magnet has to keep spinning to find its opposite pole. That's what keeps a motor moving.

WORDS to KNOW

commutator: the part of the motor that reverses the electric current.

transistor: a device that controls the flow of electricity.

Have you heard of people who commute to work? They have to travel back and forth to get there. A DC electric motor has something called a **commutator** that makes the electric current travel back and forth. It's like a metal ring split in half. Each half wraps around the part of the axle that sticks out the end of the armature.

Both sides of the commutator have a soft, springy, metal wire attached, called a brush. Each brush attaches to a positive or negative end of a power source, like a battery. Together, the commutator and brushes act as a switch. Their job is to keep shifting the magnetic field so the armature continues to spin.

Just for Fun!

What is an electrician's favorite ice cream flavor?

"Shock-o-lot!"

The Brushless DC Motor

In a simple motor, the permanent magnets are stationary and the electromagnet spins. In motors without brushes or a commutator, the permanent magnet goes inside the magnetic field of the electromagnets instead of the other way around. The trick is to change the direction of the electric current on the electromagnets at the right time to keep the permanent magnet spinning. This is done with a computer and a **transistor**, which controls the flow of electricity. It's kind of like a faucet that controls how much and how fast water comes out a tap.

Generators

An electric current can create a magnetic field. And a magnetic field can create an electric current. The same thing happens with motors. A motor uses electricity to create mechanical force, but we can reverse the action. We can use mechanical force (or motion) to turn the motor and create electricity. The machine that does this is called a generator.

turbine: a device that uses pressure on blades to spin generators and create electricity.

So how does a generator turn the armature to make electricity? Does somebody have to stand there and spin it by hand? The answer is no. It would take a lot of work to create enough electricity for a whole house or city! Generators have something called a **turbine**. It's like a wheel with wide fan blades. Pressure from many different things, like water, steam, or air, can spin the blades.

DID YOU KNOW?

The Hoover Dam on the border of Arizona and Nevada uses water from the Colorado River to push turbines. These turbines power 17 huge electrical generators that create enough electricity for over a million people.

Capacitors

You've probably played on a swing. Sometimes you need an extra push at the beginning to get moving. Then you can pump yourself to keep moving. If a motor has a big job to do like getting a furnace going or a washing machine spinning, it needs a push to get started. This extra push of electricity comes from a **capacitor**. This device stores an electrical charge until it's needed. Leyden jars were an early kind of capacitor.

Capacitors are used in almost every type of electronic gadget, from small laptops and digital cameras to big hybrid cars and MRI machines.

WORDS to KNOW

capacitor: a device that stores electrical energy until it's needed.

Nikola Tesla: Awesome Scientist

Nikola Tesla (1856–1943) was a great scientist with many ideas about electricity. He worked for Thomas Edison. The two of them got in a big argument about the best kind of current for sending out electricity. Their battle became known as "The War of Currents." Edison thought DC was better and Tesla thought AC was better.

DID YOU KNOW?

A Japanese company has built a capacitor so small that even the engineers can barely see it. It's as tiny as the period at the end of this sentence.

It turns out they were both right. Today, we use both AC and DC in our homes, buildings, appliances and electronics.

After Tesla stopped working with Edison, he began his own experiments. One of his most useful inventions was a motor without brushes or a commutator. Brushes can wear out quickly and motors without commutators run more smoothly. He discovered radio waves, developed fluorescent lighting, and helped build a power plant using the force of water from Niagara Falls.

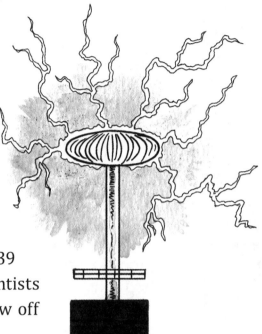

Tesla also invented what's called the Tesla coil. This large machine can produce electricity above 1,000,000 volts! It can make sparks 130 feet long (39 meters) and 300,000 watts! Today, scientists use Tesla coils to do research and to show off the power of electricity.

Nanobots

The smallest motors are found in nanobots. Nanobots are super-tiny robots. In the future, scientists hope nanobots will be able to do things like travel inside the human body and find and destroy cancer cells.

Pinwheel

When you blow on a pinwheel you are pushing on the blades with your breath. This is how a turbine works, too. Something pushes on the blades and makes them turn.

> - 4-by-4-inch square piece of paper (10 x 10 centimeters)
> - scissors
> - marker
> - ruler
> - push pin
> - pencil with eraser

1 After you cut the paper into the square, use the ruler and the marker to create a line that goes from the top left corner to the bottom right corner.

2 Make another line that goes from the bottom left corner to the top right corner. You should now have an X in the center. Mark the center of the X with a dot.

3 Cut each line. Stop 1 inch (3 centimeters) from the center dot. You should have four flaps when you're done.

4 Fold one corner of each flap over until it touches the center dot. The points should all overlap a little bit at the center.

5 Push the pin through the flap ends at the center dot and into the pencil eraser.

6 Gently blow on the blades of the pinwheel and watch them move!

Simple Motor

You can find the coated copper wire you need for this project at an electronics parts store.

CAUTION: Never strip an electrical wire yourself. Ask an adult to do it for you.

1 Ask an adult to use the wire cutter to strip about 1½ inches of the plastic insulation off each end of the 3 pieces of wire (about 4 centimeters).

2 Take one piece of wire. Leaving about 3 inches of wire at the starting end (7½ centimeters), begin wrapping the wire tightly around the battery. Leave about 3 inches at the other end too (7½ centimeters).

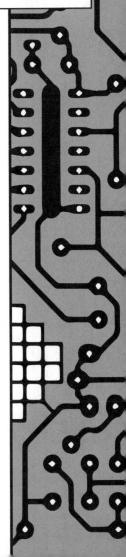

3 Carefully slide the coil you've made off the battery. Tightly twist the free ends of the wire around the loop it is touching a few times. This will keep the loops together and neat. Pull the free wires out to the sides. You should have something that looks like a circle with wire arms. This will be your winding.

4 Lay the winding on a flat surface. Use the back of a ruler or a book to flatten it as best you can. With the winding flat on the table, use the nail file to scrap the coating off of the TOP half of the wire "arms."

5 Unfold the paperclips. Straighten the bottom part but pinch the top loop closed. They should look sort of like giant needles when you're done.

CONTINUED ON NEXT PAGE . . .

Supplies:
- wire cutter
- 3 coated copper wires, each 12 inches long (30 centimeters)
- D battery
- ruler or book
- metal nail file
- 2 large paperclips
- plastic cup
- 2 ceramic magnets
- rubber band
- electrical tape

6 Turn the cup over. Hold one of the magnets against the bottom of the cup with one hand. Turn the cup back over and place the second magnet inside the cup. The two magnets will attract and hold together through the cup. Place the cup upside down on a table.

7 Stretch the rubber band around the cup, about an inch down from the magnets (2½ centimeters).

8 Slide your two paperclip loops under the rubber band, one on each side of the cup. The loops of the paperclips should be sticking up above the top of the cup.

9 Slide your winding into the paperclip loops. You want the winding to be close to, but not touching, the magnet. You may have to adjust the rubber band and paperclips to get it just right.

10 Lay your battery down on the table so the positive end is on the left and the negative end on the right. Take a second piece of wire and tape one end to the positive end of the battery. Fold the other end into a small hook. Tape one end of the last wire to the negative end of the battery and fold the other end into a small hook.

11 You're ready to hook up your motor now! Wrap the positive hook to the straight end of the left side paperclip. Wrap the negative hook to the straight end of the right side paperclip.

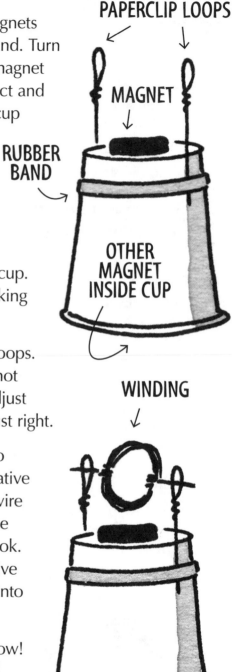

PAPERCLIP LOOPS

MAGNET

RUBBER BAND

OTHER MAGNET INSIDE CUP

WINDING

12 Give the winding a quick push. It should start spinning. If it doesn't, make sure the paperclips haven't slipped out of place. But be careful, the paperclips will be warm. You also need to make sure the winding is balanced between the paperclips. Be patient. Sometimes these motors take a bit of adjusting to get them working.

THINGS TO THINK ABOUT: How long can you get your motor to turn? Make a prediction and then test it out.

Horsepower

Engines are a certain kind of motor. They burn a fuel like gas or coal to make things move. Have you ever heard someone say an engine has good horsepower and wondered what that meant?

In late 1700s, a Scottish inventor named James Watt made an improved steam engine. Engines were pretty new and most people didn't understand what they could do. To convince people to use his engine, Watt decided to compare them to something people already knew about—horses. Watt observed horses pulling coal out of a mine and doing other work. He used his data to calculate a rate at which a horse could do in work per minute. Then he used this to describe his engine. In other words, an engine could do the same work as one horse or two horses and so forth.

Using horsepower quickly became a popular way to describe an engine's power. In terms of electricity, one horsepower (1 hp) is equal to 746 watts.

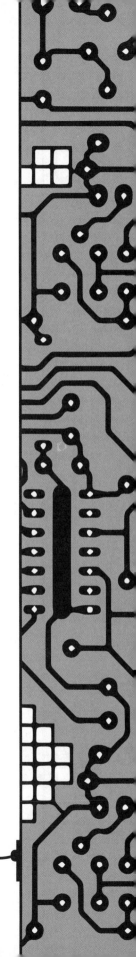

Electrophorus

An electrophorus is a simple capacitor. This project will let you carry around a static electric charge.

1 Wait for a cool, dry day. Place the pie dish face up on a table. Turn the cup over and tape it to the middle of the dish. Set this aside.

2 Turn the Styrofoam plate face down on a flat surface. Gently rub the bottom of the plate with the wool cloth for 2 minutes.

3 Pick up the pie dish using the cup as a handle. Set the bottom of the pie dish on top of the upside down Styrofoam plate.

4 Very quickly, tap the pie dish with the tip of your finger. What happens?

5 Using the cup as a handle, pick up the pie dish. If it sticks to the Styrofoam plate, use your free hand to gently pull them apart. Hold the pie dish at least 12 inches above the Styrofoam plate (30 centimeters).

SUPPLIES

- cool, dry day
- aluminum pie dish
- Styrofoam cup
- masking tape
- Styrofoam plate
- wool cloth
- stopwatch
- science journal
- pencil

ZAP!

6 Still holding the pie dish by the cup, quickly touch the dish with the tip of your finger again. What happens? Did you get another zap? Why did you get zapped when you touched the aluminum pie dish? It's because the dish is holding a charge.

7 Predict how many times you can get a zap from the pie dish and write your prediction down in your science journal. See if other people can touch the pie plate and get a shock, too.

WHAT'S HAPPENING? When you rubbed the Styrofoam plate, you gave it a negative charge. The aluminum pie dish was neutrally charged when you set it on top of the plate. When you touched the pie dish, you drew some of the electrons off. This gave the pie dish a positive charge.

Electrophorus

The electrophorus was invented in the 1760s by Alessandro Volta, who also invented the first cell battery. It got its name from the two Greek words *elektron* and *phoros*, which translate into "electricity bearer."

Earth-Friendly Electricity

We need to take care of our planet. We don't have an extra one lying around! Today, we burn a lot of **coal** to make electricity. Coal is dirty and creates tons of pollution. It is also a resource that in not **renewable**. This mean we will eventually run out and that we can't make more of it. That's why scientists are working on ways to create electricity that is Earth-friendly. They are also trying to make it easier for people to use less electricity than we do now. Both of these things will help our planet.

WORDS to KNOW

coal: a dark brown or black rock formed from decayed plants around 300 million years ago. Coal is used as a fuel.

renewable: something that isn't used up, that can be replaced.

Renewable Energy

Coal is a **natural resource** but is not renewable. A renewable resource is one that the earth makes more of all the time. For example, wind is a renewable resource. Sunshine is too.

There are many ways to use natural resources to create electricity. But nothing is perfect and each one has **advantages** and **disadvantages**.

Solar Power

Solar means sun. Solar power uses large panels that are made up of

natural resource: a material such as coal, timber, water, or land that is found in nature and is useful to humans.

advantage: something helpful.

disadvantage: something that causes difficulty or trouble.

environmental impact: harm to the environment.

smaller panels called cells. When sunlight hits the top layer of these special cells, electrons move up from the bottom layer to the top layer. This means the two layers are then charged differently. It's kind of like a battery. When the two sides are connected, electricity starts to flow.

ADVANTAGES: Solar power has little **environmental impact**. It creates zero pollution. Plus, sunlight is everywhere and it is renewable!

DISADVANTAGES: You need many panels to make enough electricity for a house and panels can be expensive. Clouds and fog can get in the way.

Hydropower

Hydro is the Greek word for water. Electricity is created when a tide, wave, or **current** pushes on a turbine. The turbine then moves a generator. The Hoover Dam in Nevada is an example of hydropower in action. So is the Itaipu Dam in South America. It sits between Paraguay and Brazil and produces the most hydroelectric power of any plant in the world. The dam provides 20 percent of Brazil's energy and almost all of Paraguay's!

ADVANTAGES: Hydropower doesn't create much pollution. It can easily produce large amounts of electricity.

DISADVANTAGES: It needs a regular source of water. Dams destroy land and can harm fish and other wildlife.

Wind Power

Sailboats and kites use wind power, of course. But how does wind turn into electricity? You've probably seen a windmill in the middle of a field. Or maybe even next to a building. Windmills use the wind to turn blades that move a generator. Like hydropower, wind power has been around for a long time.

Just for Fun!

What did the wind farm say when it met the President?

We're big fans of yours.

ADVANTAGES: Wind power has little environmental impact. In areas with strong wind, it doesn't cost much to build a windmill compared to many other energy sources.

DISADVANTAGES: The wind needs to blow around 14 miles per hour (22 kilometers per hour) for windmills to be effective. It takes many windmills to create a good amount of electricity. Some people don't like the way a windmill farm looks and windmills can be loud. Bats can get caught in the blades.

Geothermal Power

Geo means earth and *thermal* means heat. Geothermal electricity is power generated from geothermal energy, or heat made and stored inside the earth. The earth's core (or center) is very hot—around 9,000 degrees Fahrenheit (4,982 degrees Celsius)! In some places heat from deep underground turns water into steam that travels to the surface. If the steam stays trapped inside cracks or rocks thousands of feet below the earth's surface, we can drill into these areas and bring the steam up. Then we can use the steam to turn turbines and generate electricity.

ADVANTAGES: Geothermal power creates little pollution or waste.

DISADVANTAGES: Not all areas are good to drill or build a power plant on. Sometimes the earth stops making the steam.

Biomass Power

Biomass power is energy created by burning **organic** matter like wood from trees or gas from animal waste. Grass can be squeezed into bricks, a lot like the pieces of charcoal you use in a barbecue grill. When biomass is burned it can be used to heat water and create steam to turn a turbine.

ADVANTAGES: Biomass is a renewable resource and is an inexpensive way to create electricity in poorer parts of the world. It's also easy to make.

DISADVANTAGES: Biomass adds to the earth's pollution and doesn't create a lot of electricity. It is mostly used to heat homes.

Nuclear Power

Like many power plants, **nuclear** power plants use steam to power a generator. The center of atoms are split inside a container called a reactor core. This causes the atoms to release energy that heats up water and makes steam to spin the turbines.

EARTH-FRIENDLY ELECTRICITY

ADVANTAGES: Nuclear power plants can easily produce large amounts of electricity. They do not generate any air pollution.

DISADVANTAGES: An accident at a nuclear power plant can release dangerous, radioactive material into the air and ground. This can kill plants, animals and people.

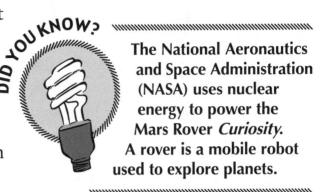

DID YOU KNOW?

The National Aeronautics and Space Administration (NASA) uses nuclear energy to power the Mars Rover *Curiosity*. A rover is a mobile robot used to explore planets.

A Career in Electrical Engineering

What do you want to do when you grow up? Now that you've learned about the fascinating world of electricity, maybe you'll choose a job in electrical engineering! Here are a few:

* Simulate and model the human brain and nervous system. These parts of the human body are all similar to electricity!

* Develop power systems for robotics that work without heavy batteries—like the ones used for the Mars rover.

* Create innovative lighting systems for airport runways that are visible in all weather conditions.

* Engineer wireless communications systems that allow Internet access from anywhere on your smart phone or tablet.

* Develop renewable energy systems from solar, wind, or wave power for remote places such as islands or satellites in space.

* Explore space, like electrical engineer Judith Resnik, who was one of the first woman astronauts. She conducted scientific experiments and operated the exterior mechanical arm, which she helped design.

Anemometer

An anemometer is a device that shows how fast the wind is blowing. You can make your own and chart wind speed at your house over time.

1 Roll the modeling clay into a mound about the size of a golf ball. Attach it to the block of wood. Push the pencil into the center of the clay with the eraser side up.

2 Glue or staple the pieces of cardboard together so that they make an X.

3 Staple a cup to the top of each end of the cardboard strips. The cups should be sideways and all facing the same way so they can catch the wind. Use the marker to color ONE of the cups red.

4 Push the pin through the middle of the cardboard X and into the pencil eraser. Gently blow on the cups to make sure they will spin.

SUPPLIES

- modeling clay
- block of wood (just about any size will work)
- pencil with an eraser
- 2 pieces of thin cardboard, 12 by 1½ inches (30 by 4 centimeters)
- glue (optional)
- stapler
- 4 small paper cups
- red marker
- flat or ball-head pin
- stopwatch
- science journal
- pencil

DID YOU KNOW?

One of the oldest and largest windmill farms is in Altamont Pass, California. It has over 4,000 windmills! But there has been so much improvement in wind turbines that 2,000 of the older turbines are being replaced with only 100 new ones.

5 Take your stopwatch, science journal, and anemometer outside. Set the anemometer in an open space where it can catch the wind.

6 Use the stopwatch to time one minute. Watch the red cup. Count how many times it completes a turn in that minute. Write the number down in your science journal.

THINGS TO THINK ABOUT:

- Does the time of day affect wind speed?

- Are some months windier than others? Test the wind speed and keep track.

- Start a scientific method worksheet and make a prediction. Then experiment. Copy the chart below into your journal and record your data.

TIME OF DAY OR MONTH	WIND SPEED

Solar **O**ven

This oven won't bake a cake but it's perfect for making s'mores!

> ⋛ shoebox with a lid
> ⋛ black paint
> ⋛ paintbrush
> ⋛ aluminum foil
> ⋛ masking tape
> ⋛ scissors
> ⋛ popsicle stick
> ⋛ graham crackers, chocolate, marshmallows
> ⋛ plastic wrap

1 Paint the outside of your box and the lid black. Let dry.

2 Line the inside of the box and the inside of the lid with aluminum foil. Make sure the shiny side is facing up. Try to keep the foil smooth and tape it to the edges.

3 Cut a flap in the box lid. The flap should be about 1 inch in from three edges of the lid (2½ centimeters). Fold the flap up and tape the loose foil to the flap.

4 Put the lid on the box. Push the flap up and use the popsicle stick to prop it open.

5 Place your solar oven in a sunny, warm place outside. It will work best on a hot day. Make sure it's not in any shade at all! Position it so the flap reflects the sun into the box.

DID YOU KNOW?

People have experimented with solar heat traps and solar ovens for centuries. It's not surprising that solar ovens were used on an expedition to Africa in the 1830s by John Herschel, because he was an astronomer. An astronomer is someone who studies the sun and stars.

6 Carefully place a graham cracker inside the box. Lay the chocolate and marshmallows on top of the graham cracker.

7 Tape a piece of plastic wrap across the opening of the box. This will help keep bugs out of the oven—and your food! It will also help trap the heat so your oven works better.

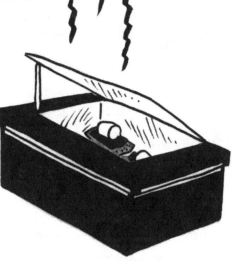

8 Wait and watch. It might take a little while for the chocolate to melt. It depends on the temperature that day and how sunny it is. Eat up and enjoy!

THINGS TO THINK ABOUT: Is there anything else you can think of to cook in your oven? This is a more energy-efficient way of making s'mores than over a campfire because it doesn't require any wood. While cooking, it does not use electricity or natural resources! And it doesn't make any pollution.

More Solar Oven Recipes

* **English Muffin Pizza:** pull apart an English muffin into two halves. Spread pizza sauce on each half. Add cheese. Place your pizzas on a napkin, paper plate, or piece of foil inside your solar oven until the cheese is melted. Enjoy!

* **Nachos:** spread out a handful of tortilla chips on a paper plate, napkin, or piece of foil. Sprinkle with shredded cheese and salsa. Place it inside your solar oven until the cheese melts. Add sour cream.

Planet Protector

Cutting back on how much electricity you use is a way for you to help the environment. And good news! There are plenty of ways you can do this. Here are 10 easy things you can start doing right away.

1 Turn off lights and electronics (like computers and stereos) when you leave a room. Encourage your family members to do the same. Put up reminder signs.

2 Encourage your family to use LED lights or help install compact fluorescent bulbs.

3 Encourage your family to use a microwave or toaster oven to cook small things instead of a big oven.

4 When it comes time to replace an appliance, help your family look for one with an Energy Star label. These appliances save electricity.

5 Keep doors closed! Heat and cool air can escape when they are open.

6 Instead of using a dryer, hang your clothes up to dry when it's sunny.

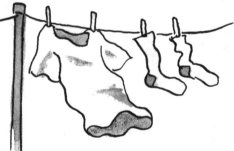

7 It takes electricity to heat and clean water at a water treatment plant. You can help cut back on energy use by taking a shower instead of a bath. Showers use less water. Also, don't let the water run while you're brushing your teeth.

8 Help plant a tree. Trees provide shade, and shade near your house means you don't need as much air conditioning.

9 Use rechargeable batteries.

10 Play outside more. Not only will you get exercise and fresh air, but you'll save electricity by not using computers, televisions, and electronic toys.

Go Green!

Have you ever heard the phrase "Go Green?" If something is "Green" it means it doesn't hurt the earth. Help spread the news about taking care of our planet. Create a poster about earth-friendly energy for your school or neighborhood.

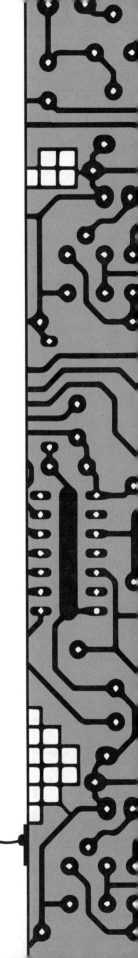

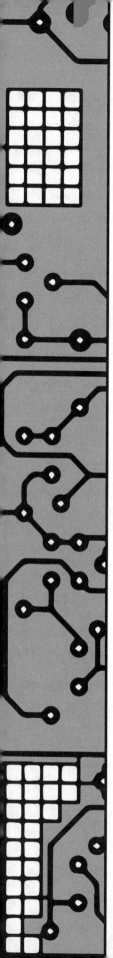

GLOSSARY

advantage: something helpful.

alternating current (AC): an electric current where electricity flows back and forth.

amber: a piece of fossilized tree sap or resin.

ampere (amp): the measurement of the amount of electric current.

anode: the end of a battery marked with a - sign.

appliance: an electrical machine used in the home, such as a toaster or washing machine.

armature: the spinning part of a motor, made of tightly coiled wires.

atmosphere: the blanket of air surrounding the earth.

atom: a small particle of matter. Atoms are the extremely tiny building blocks of everything.

axle: a rod on which something spins.

battery: a device that produces an electric current using chemicals.

BCE: put after a date, BCE stands for Before the Common Era and counts down to zero. BCE is a non-religious term that means the same thing as BC.

blackout: a loss of power.

breaker panel: the electrical box that sends electric power entering a house to each plug and switch.

capacitor: a device that stores electrical energy until it's needed.

cathode: the end of a battery marked with a + sign.

CE: put after a date, CE stands for Common Era and counts up from zero. CE is a non-religious term that means the same thing as AD.

charge: an amount of stored electricity.

chemical reaction: an event that causes the atoms of one or more kinds of matter to rearrange.

circuit: a loop that starts and finishes at the same place.

coal: a dark brown or black rock formed from decayed plants around 300 million years ago. Coal is used as a fuel.

commutator: the part of the motor that reverses the electric current.

compact fluorescent light: a light bulb that uses less electricity and lasts longer than an incandescent light bulb.

GLOSSARY

compass: an instrument that uses a magnetized needle to find north.

conductor: something that electricity moves through easily, like copper wire.

current: the steady flow of water in one direction.

diode: an electronic part that limits the flow of current to one direction.

direct current (DC): an electric current where electricity flows one direction.

disadvantage: something that causes difficulty or trouble.

disc: a round, thin piece of material.

dissect: to cut something apart to study what is inside.

electrical circuit: the pathway electricity follows.

electric current: the flow of an electrical charge through a conductor.

electricity: a form of energy caused by the movement of tiny particles. It provides power for lights, appliances, video games, and many other electric devices.

electrocution: to be injured or killed with electricity.

electrode: a conductor through which electricity enters or leaves an object like a battery.

electrolyte: a liquid or paste in a battery that allows for the flow of electric current.

electromagnet: a powerful magnet whose magnetism is turned on and off using electricity.

electromagnetism: magnetism created by a current of electricity.

electron: a particle in an atom that carries a negative charge. It is part of a shell moving around the center of an atom.

electronics: devices that use computer parts to control the flow of electricity.

energy: the ability to do things, to work.

environmental impact: harm to the environment.

expand: to spread out and take up more space.

filament: the wire used as the conducting material inside a light bulb.

force: a push or a pull.

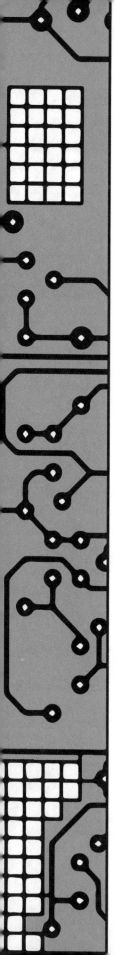

GLOSSARY

generate: to create something.

generator: a device that turns motion into electricity.

greenhouse gases: gases that trap heat in the atmosphere and make the planet warm.

hydrogen: the smallest and most plentiful atom in the universe, mostly found attached to other atoms.

incandescent: a source of electric light that works by heating a filament.

insulator: a material that prevents heat, sound, or electricity from passing through it easily.

ion: atoms or molecules with extra or missing electrons.

lightning: an electrical charge from a cloud.

lightning rod: a rod or pole used to move lightning's electrical charge safely into the ground.

load: the object that uses the electricity in a circuit.

magnet: a piece of metal that attracts metal.

magnetic field: an invisible area (or field) created by a magnet.

magnetism: a force caused by the motion of electrons that either attracts objects to it or repels them away.

matter: anything that has weight and takes up space.

mechanical: relating to machines or tools.

molecule: a group of atoms bound together by sharing electrons.

motor: a machine that turns electrical energy into motion.

natural resource: a material such as coal, timber, water, or land that is found in nature and is useful to humans.

neutral: not having a positive or negative charge.

neutron: a tiny particle inside the center of an atom that carries no charge.

nuclear: relating to energy coming from the center of an atom, called the nucleus.

organic: something that is or was living, such as wood, paper, grass, and insects.

outlet: a device in a wall that an electric cord plugs into.

GLOSSARY

oxygen: a colorless gas with no smell that makes up about one-fifth of the air around us.

parallel circuit: a circuit with a pathway to the power source for each load.

physicist: someone who studies energy and matter.

potential: something that is possible, or can develop into something real.

power: electricity made available to use.

power grid: a system of power plants and circuits.

power plant: a place where electrical power is produced to be spread out and used.

pressure: the force that pushes on an object.

proton: a tiny particle inside the center of an atom that carries a positive charge.

renewable: something that isn't used up, that can be replaced.

repel: to force away or apart.

resistance: a force that slows down another force.

resource: something that people can use.

semiconductor: a material that can be controlled to sometimes, but not always, conduct electricity.

series circuit: a circuit with a single path from the power source to the load and back to the power source.

static electricity: the buildup of an electric charge on the surface of an object.

switch: a control that opens or closes a circuit.

theory: an idea that could explain how or why something happens.

transformer: something that increases or decreases the voltage of an alternating current.

transistor: a device that controls the flow of electricity.

turbine: a device that uses pressure on blades to spin generators and create electricity.

ultraviolet light: a kind of light with short wavelengths. It can't be seen with the naked eye.

voltage (volts): the force that moves electrons in an electric current.

wattage (watts): the amount of power that's created or used.

winding: wire wrapped around an armature.

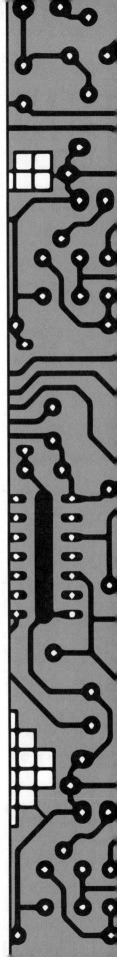

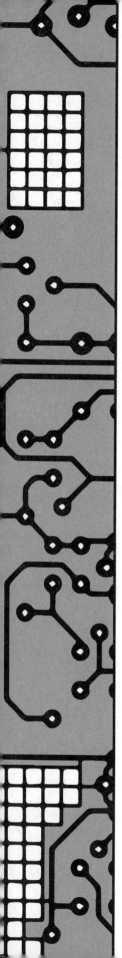

RESOURCES

Websites

Alliant Energy Kids
www.alliantenergykids.com/EnergyandTheEnvironment/
RenewableEnergy/index.htm

Bill Nye: Electric Circuits
www.youtube.com/watch?v=rg-XFXdtZnQ

Climate Kids: NASA's Eyes on the Earth
climate.nasa.gov/kids/powerupcleanly

Electricity and Circuits
www.youtube.com/watch?v=D2monVkCkX4

Electricity for Beginners
www.makemegenius.com/video_play.php?id=35

Lightning Basics
www.nssl.noaa.gov/primer/lightning/ltg_basics.html

Magnetism
www.explainthatstuff.com/magnetism.html

Nerd Girls: Ask Dr. Karen
askdrkaren.org

Nuclear Energy
library.thinkquest.org/3471/nuclear_energy.html

Start Seeing Magnetic Fields
www.evilmadscientist.com/2010/start-seeing-magnetic-fields

Tesla: Life and Legacy
www.pbs.org/tesla/ll/index.html

Try Engineering!
tryengineering.com

RESOURCES

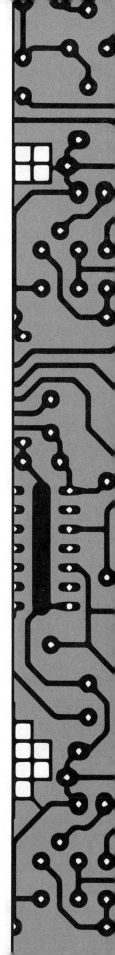

Books and Periodicals

Cole, Joanna. *The Magic School Bus and the Electric Field Trip.* New York: Scholastic Inc., 1997.

Davis, Barbara. *Science in the Real World: Why Do the Lights Turn On?* New York: Infobase Publishing, 2010.

Gardner, Robert. *Energizing Science: Projects with Electricity and Magnetism.* New Jersey: Enslow Publishers, Inc., 2006.

Goldsworthy, Kaite. *Electricity.* New York: AV(@) by Weigl, 2012.

Graf, Mike. *How does a Waterfall Become Electricity*? Illinois: Raintree, 2009.

Johnson, George. *"Chasing Lightning."* National Geographic, August 2012.

Kessler, Colleen. *A Project Guide to Electricity and Magnetism.* Delaware: Mitchell Lane Publishers, 2012.

Leavitt, Amie Jane. *Who Really Discovered Electricity?* Minnesota: Capstone Press, 2011.

Monroe, Ronald. *What are Electrical Circuits?* New York: Crabtree Publishing Company, 2012.

Mullins, Lisa. *Inventing the Electric Light.* New York: Crabtree Publishing Company, 2007.

Parker, Steve. *Eyewitness Electricity.* New York: DK Publishing, Inc.,1992.

Parker, Steve. *Electricity and Magnetism.* Wisconsin: Gareth Stevens Publishers, 2007.

Woodford, Chris. *Routes of Science: Electricity.* Michigan: Thomson Gale, 2004.

INDEX

INDEX

INDEX